ANYONE CAN BE HEALED

CECELIA WOODARD

Unless otherwise noted, all scripture quotations are from The Hebrew-Greek Key Study Bible KJV.

Scripture taken from The Hebrew-Greek Key Study Bible, Old and New Testament © copyright 1984 and 1991 Spiros Zodhiates and AMG International, Inc. dba AMB Publishers.

This book is a work of non-fiction. All names are used by permission.

All rights reserved. No parts of this book may be reproduced in any form, without permission in writing from the author.

Chosen To Write Publishing LLC books may be ordered through booksellers or by contacting the Publisher.

Copyright © 2012 Cecelia Woodard
ISBN-10: 0989540545
ISBN-13: 978-09895405-4-4
Jackson, Mississippi

Chosen To Write Publishing LLC
3315 Delphos Avenue
Dayton, OH 45417
(937) 607-1585
http://ctwpublishing.com

Printer:
CreateSpace

Cover Designer:
AL-Lamontau Brooks

Printed in the United States

DEDICATION

To my mother, Jean Webster, who has gone home to be with the Lord.

To my son, Eugene Ragland, who is my gift from God. You belong to God; there is a Kingdom builder in you.

My grandsons, Courtney Younger and Donte Belcher, you are God's chosen.

My granddaughter, Isis (who I call Deborah, a woman of balance) – call those things that are not as though they were.

To my aunts, Joan Ragland and Joyce Ragland, thank you for loving on me.

To my aunt, Ernestine Denning, who went home to be with the Lord and helped guide me through life. Each one of you pushed me to believe in myself when I did not. There were always words of encouragement when things looked bad. Thank you for being there through all of my trials and tribulations.

To all of my many, many, many cousins, I love you.

Prophetess Cecelia Woodard

ANYONE

CAN BE HEALED

CECELIA WOODARD
An Incredible Journey of Physical Healing and Wholeness

ANYONE CAN BE HEALED

CONTENTS

	Forward	vi
	Acknowledgments	vii
	Encouragement	viii
1	My First Encounter With The Lord	13
2	Seventeen and Pregnant	15
3	The Drug Stage	18
4	The Devil's Plan Was Canceled	23
5	Recovery	27
6	The Set Up	30
7	Total Healing	33
8	Great Is His Faithfulness	35
9	Deliverance Without A Trace	38
	TESTIMONIALS OF HEALINGS	43
	VICTORY OVER FEAR SCRIPTURES	51
	SCRIPTURES FOR HEALING	54
	NOTES SECTION	57

CECELIA WOODARD

FORWARD

God has truly blessed this great woman of God, Dr. Cecelia Woodard. I have known her for 30 years. I have watched her life develop through many obstacles. Reading this spiritual account of the healing power of God through a chosen vessel, will only prove to you, that God can do anything, but fail.

It has been my pleasure for more than 20 years, to been given the assignment to be Pastor and Bishop as a guide for what God has anointed Dr. Woodard to do. The prophetic word that comes from her is documented to be accurate and on point. This woman has walked with God and very carefully moves when directed by God.

I could say much more, but read for yourself what God has given her to give to you.

Be blessed tremendously in Jesus' name.

Yours because of the perfect sacrifice,
Bishop Charles R. Lyles
Victory First Presbyterian Deliverance Church
Atlantic City, New Jersey

ANYONE CAN BE HEALED

ACKNOWLEDGMENTS

I give honor to God, and only God, for this book. For in Him we live, and move, and have our being; (Acts 17:28(a), KJV partial).

I would like to take this time to honor my Bishop Dr. Charles R. Lyles and Pastor Dr. Diana L. Lyles for their continued support over the years. For inspiring me to be all that I can be through their preaching, teaching, rebukes, encouragement, but most of all their love that pulled me from membership to daughtership. Thank you for loving me. (Even when I was a runaway child, running wild).

Pastor Kenneth Thomas, my prayer partner, you helped me through when I did not know which way was up. Love you big time!!! (I worked your nerves, but the Lord kept them – smile).

Pastors Liz and Warner Taylor who continues to be there for me in Dayton, Ohio. Charity and Faith Thru Jesus Christ Sanctuary, I love you guys, you're the best (Pastor Warner, I am on my way to my Cosmos blessings, you spoke it!!!).

My buddy Evangelist/Author Audrey Green (Aud) love you, girl.

Thank you Prophet Trumbo for the prophetic insight concerning the writing of this book.

To my spiritual daughter, Prophetess LaShonda Trumbo, who always says, "Mom, you can do it".

To all the Prophets that spoke over me saying, "God said write that book", for allowing God to use them to push me to the next level and to finally settle down and finish the book.

To Prophetess Dr. Linda Taylor, my god-sister and prayer partner: (We have come a long way from sitting on the curb together as children on the Westside of Atlantic City, New Jersey).

To Pastor Gwen Dawud and her husband Jamal "Doc" Dawud (watch those haircuts) whose house, wherever they go, is my house.

Thank you, Bishop Dixon for all of your advice and prayers and for pushing me in spite of.

To Pastor Michelle Fields, what can I say? You know how to make a praise break happen!

To everyone who had a part in the writing of this book, thank you.

I humble myself to you and I thank you for your love, prayers and support over the years.

CECELIA WOODARD

ENCOURAGEMENT

ANYONE CAN BE HEALED

Dear Reader

This book will touch every soul . . . because it is a true story . . . as told by one of God's anointed, and powerful vessels in the person of Dr. Cecelia Woodard, Founder and Pastor of WIN International Ministries.

The names have not been changed, because God Himself blesses all who will come and believe. Come now and read this wonderful story. You will be connected to the truth that only the Word of God can reveal. You will become one of the many who, after reading this powerful work, will know that "Anyone Can Be Healed" to the Glory of God!

To Prophetess Woodard,

As my Pastor, I am so blessed to see you lead us to the next level in God . . . In Faith . . . In Christ . . . In Holiness . . . As we build the Kingdom of God.

Founder of Daddy God Ministries
Prophet Kenneth L. Thomas, Sr.
Houston, Texas

CECELIA WOODARD

A Story of Courage

As I read this book, I cried, laughed and realized that with God all things are possible. When faced with decisions, the Lord will always direct ones path. For those seeking healing, deliverance, hope and love, put your trust in the Lord.

Prophetess Woodard's testimony is one of courage, love and persistence. The Lord pulled her out of the pit of sin and strategically placed her into His life of joy. I recommend this book to anyone in need of an anointed testimony.

Audrey Green
Evangelist/Author
Dayton, Ohio

ANYONE CAN BE HEALED

Powerful

Prior to founding EWM International, I spent many years traveling with internationally recognized Evangelists. These great men and women of God would allow me to accompany them from city to city, whether it was a church or a stadium. Night after night, we watched in amazement as the Holy Spirit drew throngs of people to the meetings. Those were wearying days and nights, but I'll never forget the expressions on the faces of people whose lives were touched by the power of God.

Some of you may not know that many of these great men and women, were moving in miraculous ministries of signs and wonders long before their churches and ministries became nationally and globally known. To this day, many of those same men and women continue to stand before multitudes transforming the lives of many.

That is why I am not at all surprised that Prophetess Cecelia Woodard, has authored such a powerful book about healing.

Prophetess Woodard has not written just a theoretical work, her personal observation and experience highlight the trust you are about to read. Anyone Can Be Healed will inspire many Christians to a new level of faith. Through it they will believe that God can and will use them to bring the miraculous to a generation that desperately needs to be reached with the power of God.

Dr. E'Vann Walker
Las Vegas, Nevada

CECELIA WOODARD

This Book Is The Timing Of God

This book has come at a time such as this. The people of God need to know that God can and will use anyone who is willing to surrender to His will and original plan for mankind to eternally establish the Kingdom of God in the earth.

Winsome Stewart
Chicago, IL

ANYONE CAN BE HEALED

1

MY FIRST ENCOUNTER WITH THE LORD

My first encounter with the Lord happened around the age of ten years old. A school mate, Pauline Plummer, and I used to walk to school almost every day. She was, and still is very much into Holiness. She is now an anointed Pastor in Atlantic City, New Jersey. She wore long skirts and dresses (no pants) and was not allowed to do any of the things that we who were not saved did. Me, being the curious person that I am, would ask her all the time, why couldn't she do what I did or dress the way I dressed. Pauline, being who she was, (saved) always gave the same answer, "I am saved." When I would ask her what did that mean, her answer was always the same, "Come to church and see". Of course my response was always, "No". I used to playfully tease her and call her Holy Roller. Well, now the jokes on me. I am now a "Holy Roller", thank you, Jesus!

One morning on our way to school she asked me to go to church with her that night. This time I said, "Yes". I did not know why at that time, but now I understand it all. I cannot tell you what the message was about. I was too busy watching people fall on the floor in the Spirit of God, speaking in tongues and dancing in the Spirit. Now I am falling on the floor, speaking in tongues and dancing in the Spirit of God. What I do know is, that when the altar call was made, somehow was at the altar.

Being ten years old, not really understanding what was going on, when I was asked if I wanted to be baptized, I said "Yes". Everyone else was going to be baptized, so I did it too. Not realizing at that time, it was my first real day on earth, the day I was reborn. As you know, growing up is a learning experience. So that night I got baptized. Trust me, the water was make-your-teeth chatter, body-shivering cold. After getting dressed, my friend's mother, Pastor Louise Burch, (she was not a Pastor then, but she was used mightily of God to change lives) told me that I would never be the same.

Of course, I had no idea what she was talking about. I went from that day on, business as usual in my ten-year-old life and teenage years until the age of seventeen. That is when things began to really get crazy. As you enter in and read about my life, you will understand, that when I say that God was with me, He was and still is with me.

ANYONE CAN BE HEALED

2

SEVENTEEN AND PREGNANT

At the age of seventeen, I got pregnant. Twice a week, starting at my fifth month, I would become very sick. The doctor said the sickness and the repeated false labor that I was experiencing were normal. In the seven and a half month of my pregnancy, I became severely ill: head swimming, stomach cramping to the point I could barely stand up and was vomiting. My best friend, at that time, took me to the hospital. After checking me, they sent me home again. While in the hospital lobby, waiting for a taxi to take us home, I became violently ill again. The hospital personnel insisted this was normal and still refused to admit me or give me a more thorough examination. No one took my temperature or blood pressure, either at that time.

Thank God for a praying grandmother. I remember her calling the Unity Prayer Group that night to pray for me. She had me to sleep in her room that night and she sat on the edge of her bed and rocked and prayed for me all that night. She was very worried because the vomiting would not stop. Eventually, there was nothing left to come up. In the middle of the night, I was gripped with pain that was actually worse than having the baby. I was in such agony; so much so that the paramedics could not pull my legs straight to put me on the stretcher. Somehow, they got me on it. My temperature was so high it scared the paramedics.

Once at the hospital, because of my high temperature, they had to cool me down right away. They had to get it down fast and be careful in doing so because of the baby. After examining me, the doctor said my appendix had to be removed. Tubes were everywhere: in my arms for the IV, in my nose for any poisons in my system, and in my stomach to feed the baby. At one point, they didn't know if the surgery could be done without risking one of us. They could not put me under, so they did a spinal and I had to sit very still. Believe me, it was extremely difficult to do because of the severe pain from the contractions.

After they removed my appendix, I had to stay in the hospital for the rest of the pregnancy. There was concern about the stitches breaking loose or something else going wrong. The doctor told me later that during the surgery they were uncertain as to which one of us would survive: the baby or me. But look at God, answering the prayers of a grandmother. **James 5:16 KJV - The effectual fervent prayer of a righteous man availeth much.**

The praying grandmother brought two generations through: her granddaughter and her great grandson. God gave the doctors the wisdom and the knowledge of what to do and how to do it. Mothers, grandmothers, fathers, grandfathers, stay on your posts. We need you. For those in the body of Christ who do not have a biological praying parent or parents, do not despair. Mothers in Zion, stay there. You are needed more than ever.

So, there I was seventeen and a mother that did not have a clue. Thank God for my immediate family and grandparents. Young ladies, stay saved. You are not ready to be mothers. Your salvation is not worth a short 'feel good'. Your salvation is not worth a boyfriend who only wants your body and not your hand in marriage when you both are ready. God will keep you if you stay focused. When it is time, the Lord will bless you with the right one. **Proverbs 18:22 KJV – Whoso findeth a wife findeth a good thing, and obtaineth favour of the Lord.** Let that man find you so that you can be his good thing AND his blessing.

ANYONE CAN BE HEALED

I was not saved when I had my son but the Lord blessed me with a loving, supportive family. Everyone is not so blessed. The club, ladies and young ladies, is not where the party is. The real party is in the house of God.

3

THE DRUG STAGE

In the summer of 1968, my boyfriend introduced me to marijuana. For a while, that was the only drug that I did. Then slowly, I began to experiment with other drugs: LSD on the sugar cube, Paper Acid, PCP, Microdot, and Angel Dust, just to name a few. I tried most of the hallucinogens that were out there at that time. Thank God for my Aunt Claudette who we called Aunt Choocie. She would keep my son for days at a time.

My aunts and grandparents helped raise my son while I was running around out of my mind on drugs. I need to say that when I gave my life to the Lord, I had to apologize to my son and ask for his forgiveness because I was not there as a mother for him during that time in my life. I had to have his forgiveness because he went through unnecessary trauma due to my foolishness.

Parents, apologize to your children for any hurt that you may have caused them due to various forms of neglect. Let healing begin in that area. Some of our children are out of control because they are hurting and don't know how to stop the pain. We have to encourage healing through Christ

ANYONE CAN BE HEALED

Jesus. My son and I are now healed and whole in that area. Yes, we are fighting other demons but not that one. He wrote me a letter and said he would not trade me in for anything in this world. My baby boy made me cry but they were tears of joy and healing, not just for me, but for us.

I do not think my family knew the extent of my drug use. They just thought I was running the streets. But little did they know, I would do speed and stay gone two to three days at a time. I would have to take downers to come down from the speed high so that I could sleep. There was a point in time that I was so high, I lost three days of my life. I cannot tell you, even right now, who I was with, where I was or how I got home. All I know is that there are three days missing out of my life that I cannot account for to this day.

In the beginning of this book, I stated that the night I was baptized, Evangelist Burch spoke over me and said that I would never "be the same". That word which was spoken over me that night, kept me those three days until it was time for me to come into the Body of Christ. Between the prophecy and the manifestation, you have to go to the potter's house and be made on the wheel. I was on the wheel all those years and I am still on it. When I was driving behind the wheel of a car, drugged out my mind, God kept me. Some days, I would smoke marijuana laced with opium or hashish. It was nothing to wake up in the morning and smoke a joint, and then take a tab of acid or do some chocolate mescaline, which is a type of speed.

Through it all, God kept my mind. The song says, "When I think of the goodness of Jesus and all He has done for me". **Ephesians 1:4-7 KJV - According as he hath chosen us in him before the foundation of the world, that we should be holy and without blame before him in love: having predestinated us unto the adoption of children by Jesus Christ to himself, according to the good pleasure of his will, to the praise of the glory of his grace, wherein he hath made us accepted in the beloved. In whom we have redemption through his blood, the forgiveness of sins, according to the riches of his grace.**

This is a good place to get my dance on; it was His good pleasure to keep my mind. I did not suffer any damage to my electrolytes. My neurological system was kept intact. I did not end up in an institution from taking so much acid. I never had a bad trip and I did not see things that were not there. When people around me were hallucinating, I wanted to see what they were seeing, so I would take more acid, in addition to the acid that I had already taken.

There was a phase when cough syrup was the "thing to do". My son's godmother and I bought a bottle one night and decided to try it. She drank one half and I drank the other. Needless to say, after we were done being sick, we never tried that again. Two nights later, a young man in the club where we were partying, drank the same kind of cough syrup that we did. About an hour later, his nose started to bleed. It could not be stopped and he was rushed to the hospital. His blood pressure went up so high he hemorrhaged through his nose and died. The song says, "When I look back over my life, and I begin to think things over, I have a testimony". To this day, I have never had a flashback and I was eating acid like children eat M&M candy. **Jeremiah 1:5 KJV - Before I formed thee in the belly I knew thee; and before thou camest forth out of the womb I sanctified thee, and I ordained thee a prophet unto the nations.**

When God has His hand on you, you may go through, but you are coming out with victory. I never had just one single addiction. I did not like just one drug: I liked a variety of drugs, acid, PCP, etc. I never liked heroine (it made me itch) nor cocaine for its cost was too expensive.

My acid days were from 1968 – 1970. It was the time of Woodstock, Jimi Hendrix, the Beatles and the Motown sound. In the words of the Isley Brothers, it was a time of, "it's your thing, do what you want to do". I was a hippie: free love and all. Don't sit in the judgment seat over that statement. We all have a testimony. If more people would tell the real story, a lot of church folk could and would be delivered. We won't tell who we really were in the world. We do not want to be associated with certain groups of people now that we are on the Lord's side. Some of us were out there with the lesbians, homosexuals, pimps and whores. Some of those same friends that I was out there with are in jail for murder. During those times, I did not realize that it was the hand of God on my life. Even in my sin state, God

ANYONE CAN BE HEALED

was there with me all the time. **Romans 5:8 KJV - But God commendeth his love toward us, in that, while we were yet sinners, Christ died for us.**

After a while, acid was not an attraction for me anymore. At the end of 1970, wondering what to do with my life (I still had a son to raise), I went into the Job Corps. I started from the Job Corps Center in Jersey City, New Jersey. It was there that I was blessed to meet Shirley Chisholm, who encouraged the young black women and men to learn and grow. After six months at Jersey City, I transferred to another Job Corps Center in Albuquerque, New Mexico. Because of my grades, I was able to go to college at the University of New Mexico and study Criminal Justice. I did one semester, maintaining a "B" average.

While there, I met some very influential people. Andrew Young was one of them. We sat and spoke on more than one occasion at the Black Student Union at the University of New Mexico, of which I was the President. He poured so many valuable words of wisdom into me during those times, but I was not ready, marijuana had stepped back into the picture.

Restless, I transferred again. This time I went to Charleston, West Virginia Job Corps Center. While there I really settled into my studies. Because my grades were still so good, I was one of the few that was chosen to attend West Virginia State on a full scholarship. By this time, I had stopped smoking marijuana and continued to major in Criminal Justice, maintaining a "B" average. My goal was to become a Corporate attorney, but halfway through my next semester, marijuana once again became part of my life and the party started all over again. Young people, if you're reading this, don't believe the "HYPE", stay off drugs and stay in school. **1 Peter 5:8 NKJV - Be sober, be vigilant; because your adversary the devil walks about like a roaring lion, seeking whom he may devour.**

After learning my skill as an Administrative Assistant at the Job Corps Center in Charleston, West Virginia, I returned home to Atlantic City. Upon returning home, I was disappointed that it seemed while I was gone, nothing much had changed. I was in the Job Corps from 1970 to 1972. I

CECELIA WOODARD

then entered the United States Air Force. After four years in the military, I returned home, again, nothing much had changed. Instead of using my Administrative and Accounting skills, I started smoking marijuana and doing speed again. Since I rejoined negative people, places and things, it was not long before I entered back into the cycle of drugs and did not accomplish anything constructive.

ANYONE CAN BE HEALED

4

THE DEVIL'S PLAN WAS CANCELED

During the summer of 1976, I met someone and entered into what I did not know at that time, would be an abusive relationship. After my ex and I broke up, I moved back to Atlantic City from Pennsylvania. My ex would call me constantly and ask me to come back and talk things out. Tired of the phone calls, I agreed to go to Pennsylvania to talk things out even though in my mind it was over. After hanging up the phone a strange feeling came over me, as if to say, "don't go". I shook it off, thinking it was just me.

The next day, while on the bus, that same uneasy feeling came over me and again I brushed it off. When I got off the bus, I heard a voice say, "Get back on the bus and go home". The voice was so loud I looked around to see who was speaking to me. Since I did not see anyone that I knew who could have spoken to me, I sat in the waiting area of the bus station for my ex to pick me up. In a short while, he came and we went to his mother's house that evening. But instead of talking, we ended up going to a club. However, before we went to the club, while at the house, there was just about any kind of drug that you could have wanted. Any other time, I would have helped myself, but this night, I just wanted to have our talk and go home. After my ex and I had our talk, I was ready to go. My mind was made up, and I was not going to go back into an abusive relationship.

CECELIA WOODARD

The hour had grown late, and I had missed that last bus back to Atlantic City. Therefore, I agreed to go to the club. I planned to then get the bus in the morning to return home. (The club closed at 6:00 in the morning.)

As the evening went on, that strange feeling that something was going to happen came over me, and again I brushed it off. Just as the club was about to close, I remember saying to myself, "Girl, you were worried about nothing", then it happened. Just as I reached for my coat, my ex shot me almost point blank, aiming for my face. Because I was reaching for my coat, my arm and face were angled to the side. The bullet hit my arm first. It went through my upper arm, in and out of my collarbone, (without shattering anything – Thank You, Jesus) and into my jawbone on the right side of my face. I did not see, hear or feel anything, when I was shot. I do remember being in a dark dense place. I cannot say that it was hell, and I cannot say that it was not. I cannot explain the darkness to you, because there is nothing on earth to compare it to. Suddenly, this scripture became real to me: **Psalm 91:11-12 KJV - For He shall give His angels charge over thee, to keep thee in ALL thy ways. They shall bear thee up in their hands, lest thou dash thy foot against a stone.**

Next, I heard what sounded like a loud bell in my ear, and eventually I became aware that people were screaming. I was told that as I was about to fall to the floor, I started standing back up, as if something or someone was pulling me up, like a puppet on a string. I cannot remember all that was going on in those few seconds, but what I do know is that I never hit the floor. When I came to myself, and saw that I was covered in blood, I thought someone next to me had gotten shot. While not realizing it, I was holding my face. I was trying to figure out why everyone was looking at me. That's when I was told that I had been shot. The disc jockey wanted to carry me to the car, but that same voice that I had heard in the bus station said, "Walk to the car". I cannot explain it, but as I was walking to the car, I regained my strength, and did not feel faint as I did in the beginning.

When we arrived at the hospital, while everyone was running around looking for a wheelchair, I got out of the car and walked into the emergency room. I approached a nurse to get help and told her that I was the one that

ANYONE CAN BE HEALED

she was getting the wheelchair for. I was told later that the reason for my calmness was because I was in shock. But looking back, it was ALL GOD.

The bullet entered my right upper arm, came out of my collarbone and went into my jaw and rested behind my right ear. The doctors took X-ray after X-ray, looking for bone chips and bullet fragments. They could not understand why there was not more damage to my arm especially because of how the bullet went in my arm and came out of my collarbone. Where the bullet entered my arm, everything should have been shattered.

My right arm should be useless but again nothing vital was hit, going in or coming out. Look at the work of God. The bullet made a clean entry and a clean exit. Nothing was chipped, cracked or broken.

My right eye was paralyzed open and the nerves were severed at the bullet entry point on the right side of my face. As a result, my face was twisted toward the left the next morning. The doctors said that I would be like that the rest of my life. They elected to leave the bullet embedded in my head because it was in too deep to risk removing it. I attended speech therapy for a year. I had to learn how to talk without slurring my words, and how to pronounce words with P's, S's, and F's, so that I could be understood. I needed to settle down and learn to live with this. For a year, I could not taste or smell food. I had to remember what foods tasted and smelled like.

We often take the small things for granted like tasting food, smelling coffee or blinking an eye. When those small things are suddenly gone, you truly understand, that it was "God who made us, and not we ourselves". **Psalm 100:3 KJV – Know ye that the Lord he is God: it is he that hath made us, and not we ourselves; we are his people, and the sheep of his pasture.**

WE have not power of our own. I could not make my face go back to normal. I could not make my eye blink. I could not make my taste buds work or tell my sense of smell to return. BUT GOD, BUT GOD, BUT GOD. This is a good place to dance!

My ex did not go to jail for shooting me. Because the bullet was still in my face and the gun was thrown away, there was no evidence. As time went on, my mind went into payback mode. I believe the Lord fought my battle

CECELIA WOODARD

so that I did not have to. Eventually, he went to prison for a long time due to unrelated crimes he had committed.

ANYONE CAN BE HEALED

5

RESTORATION

One morning in 1980, I was eating scrambled eggs and I began to feel very strange. That same voice I had heard a year earlier said, "Don't be afraid, get up and go to the hospital". When the Lord sets things up, He sets things up!

When I walked into the emergency room, there was no one there. No intake person to register me, no one, not even a person waiting for medical attention. An emergency room is normally booming with activity, but it was quiet and oddly serene for an emergency room. While standing there, a doctor came around the corner and I told him I needed help. Now watch the move of GOD. After explaining to the doctor about the bullet in my face and how I was feeling, the doctor, himself, took me to the X-ray room. He took the X-ray, put me in a room in the ER and told me to wait. (like I was going someplace, also remember, I had not been registered) and he had the film developed right away. The Lord broke protocol just for me. Doctors don't take X-rays, they have an X-ray tech do it. **DON'T TELL ME THAT GOD CAN'T BREAK PROTOCOL JUST FOR YOU.** He worked outside the laws of nature to have a raven that eats rotten food, bring good food to the prophet. **Kings 17:4 KJV - And it shall be, that**

CECELIA WOODARD

thou shall drink of the brook; and I have commanded the ravens to feed thee there.

Even though at that time, I was not saved, the Lord had the doctor there just for me. After the doctor came and showed me the X-ray, he explained that the bullet had dislodged from the bone.

During the previous year of speech therapy, I kept asking the therapist for something to get rid of the scar tissue, because of the terrible itching. I do not know if the scar tissue was causing the itching or not, I just wanted some relief. The more I asked, the more he said no. There is an injection that can dissolve scar tissue to a degree. But I know now the scar tissue was in the plan of God.

When the bullet came out of the bone, the scar tissue acted like a cradle and kept the bullet from touching the nerves. If the bullet had rested on the nerves, it would have done more damage in the area of my neck and jaw and would have caused excruciating pain.

Now, back to the emergency room. After he showed me on the X-ray where the bullet was laying, he scheduled an appointment for me to be seen at the surgical clinic the next day. After being examined at the clinic, I was scheduled for surgery. Two weeks later, I went in for the surgery. A team of about ten doctors came to see me. There was an oral surgeon because I had a hairline fracture to the jaw, a plastic surgeon to make my smile normal, and two neurosurgeons to reconnect the severed nerves. Well, let me tell you, none of those doctors were in God's plan.

When it came time for the surgery, because it was near the holidays, there was no operating room available. Some of the staff had taken days off due to the New Year holidays, so the operating room was not at full staff. Ultimately, I was sent home and rescheduled for February 3, 1980. What was supposed to be an eight to ten hour operation, was only 20 minutes long. The surgeon said, as soon as he made the incision, the bullet was right there. All he had to do was take it out. The surgeons decided not to take any further action to repair my face or nerves (again God's hand) and I was home the next day. I do not know if I can express in words how I felt. I was in awe of the move of God once again. I experienced unexplainable joy in my spirit knowing the bullet was gone. A

ANYONE CAN BE HEALED

sweet peace settled in my soul and a weight lifted, knowing that I could sleep without fear that the bullet would shift as I was sleeping.

Two weeks later, I went back to get the stitches removed. While there, I explained to the doctor that I was having sharp shooting pains in my head. He said that I would have those pains for the rest of my life because of the nerve damage.

# CECELIA WOODARD

6

THE SET UP

    After I left the doctor's office, I went to meet a friend for lunch. He had been witnessing to me about the Lord and became my husband eight months later. He was doing some repair work at the church where he was serving. I later joined that fellowship also. But that day, while sitting in the church waiting for him to finish what he was doing, I reached for the Bible that was on the seat next to me. I do not know what I turned to. I was thinking about what the doctor said to me. I did not want to have hot, searing pains scorching through my head for the rest of my life. The tears started to make their escape down my cheeks. For the first time since I had gotten shot, I released a year of pain because of the anguish I had suffered over the past twelve months. What a mighty God we serve! He healed me from a year of torment in twenty minutes. I had never known that kind of love or healing from a God that I had heard about, but never experienced until that moment. The relief was overwhelming. The joy, unspeakable.

    At this point in my life, I still had not given my life to the Lord – but look at His love for me. **Romans 5:8 KJV - But God commendeth his own love toward us, in that, while we were yet sinners, Christ died for us.**

    To me, my face felt the same, but I was not the same. When I looked in the mirror, I saw a mouth twisted toward the side of my face and a right eye that wouldn't obey the command to close. My eye constantly ran be-

ANYONE CAN BE HEALED

cause the tear duct was damaged and I had to wear an eye patch. Since I could not close the lid, my eye was always exposed. The patch protected the eye and kept out foreign objects. Without the patch, anything could have flown into my eye and blinded me or caused a serious infection. Let me tell you, I was a real mess! The song says, "God specializes" and He specialized in my mess!

While I was sitting in the church getting emotionally healed, I felt someone standing next to me. When I looked up, it was the Pastor of the church, Pastor Loretta Farmer. She did not say anything to me at first; she just started to pray.

After praying, she witnessed to me about the Lord and asked me if I wanted to be saved and baptized. I said 'Yes'. She asked me to come back that night to be baptized (she had several people being baptized that evening).

Remember, earlier in the book, I said that my friend's mother told me I would never be the same, after I was baptized at the age of ten in her church, full circle. At this point, I forgot all about lunch. I went home to prepare to be baptized. I dressed in my jeans, put a bag of marijuana in my pocket and went to be baptized. After the baptism, my plan was to go to the club, get high and party. After leaving the baptism, I found myself putting the key in the door to my house and not venturing out to the club. I said to myself, "What are you doing at home and not at the club?" It was like the Lord took the thought of the club completely away from me. **Isaiah 55:8-9 KJV - For my thoughts are not your thoughts, neither are your ways my ways, saith the Lord. For as the heavens are higher than the earth, so are my ways higher than your ways, and my thoughts than your thoughts.**

I had left the club in the baptismal water, asthma in the water (born with it, have not had an attack since I got baptized), cigarettes in the water, marijuana smoking in the water. I did not realize all that had happened to me until the next day. **2 Corinthians 5:17 KJV - Therefore, if any man be in Christ, he is a new creature: old things are passed away; behold, all things are become new.**

CECELIA WOODARD

Two months after giving my life to the Lord, I was filled with His Spirit. I had never felt so loved in my whole life as I did the night I received the Holy Ghost.

ANYONE CAN BE HEALED

7

TOTAL HEALING

As I said, later in the year of 1979, that same brother who witnessed to me about the Lord, became my husband. He was and still is a union plumber and was on a job in Atlantic City at the time of our marriage. During those times, we would stay at my mother's house. One night I had a dream that I was playing and laughing with a baby, under a bright light. I had never seen a light so bright but soft at the same time. I was smiling and winking my eye. The more I winked my eye in the dream, the more the baby laughed.

I woke up out of the dream abruptly. I thought about the dream, saying to myself, "I can't wink my eye". After taking a shower, I thought I had forgotten to wash my face. As I was about to wash it, I thought, I did wash my face. The same voice that I had heard so many times before said, "Splash plain water on your face and look in the mirror". I cannot explain it but when I looked in the mirror before I showered, my face was twisted. After splashing the water on my face and looking in the mirror as the voice had commanded me to do, my face was normal. Then the voice said, "Wink". I WINKED! My tear duct was healed as well. I did not know it then, but it was the voice of God that had been speaking to me each time I was given divine guidance. I started crying, rejoicing, running around the house, screaming and speaking in tongues. When my husband came home, I hugged him so hard I was almost choking him. As I was telling him what had happened, he grabbed my face between his hands and started giving God praise. He was crying more than I was. We had some serious praise in that house that night.

CAN'T NOBODY DO YOU LIKE JESUS!

A month later, I was walking down the street and noticed a pleasant odor of food. (Remember, I had lost the ability to taste and smell. I was eating from memory). At first, I did not notice it until I walked passed a bakery and I smelled the bread. If you have never lost your sense of smell, you cannot understand what it was like to be able to smell again after more than a year. I went and sat on the beach and enjoyed the aroma of the ocean air, and gave God the Glory for what He had done. Before I could think what next, you got it, a week later my ability to taste was restored. I was eating and suddenly, I was actually tasting the food. Let me tell you, I went crazy tasting things. Look at the healing power of God. **Jeremiah 32:27 KJV - Behold, I am the Lord, the God of all flesh: is there anything too hard for me?**

We must remember, He is the one who wakes us up each morning. He is the one who gives us the use and activity of our limbs. It is because of Him we live, and move and have our being.

It was because of God that the bullet did not hit anything vital in my upper arm and when it came out of my collarbone there were no bone chips. The doctors said they had never seen a neater entrance or exit of a bullet wound in that area at that time. I was not saved when I got shot. So therefore, it was not because I was serving God. Our righteousness is like filthy rags to God anyway. It was the grace of God who answered the prayers of an interceding grandmother. When you are chosen by God, the devil cannot stop the plan of salvation for your life. God stayed the hand of death. It is God, and Him alone, who has the power to heal, set free and deliver.

ANYONE CAN BE HEALED

8

GREAT IS HIS FAITHFULNESS

In the year of 1986, I was set free from an abusive marriage. He went to jail for double rape. That's another book. Yes, the same man that witnessed to me about the Lord, did this terrible thing. I moved back to Atlantic City and joined Victory First Presbyterian Deliverance Church, where Bishop Charles R. Lyles and Pastor Diana L. Lyles are the Leaders. It is under their leadership that I continue to serve, and receive further instruction from the Word of God. SIDE BAR: No matter how anointed you are or what your calling is, it is never greater than your leader or leaders. When you have anointed leaders that are teaching and living what they teach and preach, YOU STAY THERE. I thank God for the God in them, and their prayers over the many years. As you read these last chapters, you will understand how important it is to stay under anointed leadership.

In 1990, there was a drive to donate blood to the Red Cross at the job where I was working. I participated and a week later I received a letter from the Red Cross informing me that there was a possibility that I had Hepatitis C (HCV), and to take the letter with the lab results to my doctor. My doctor arranged for me to have a biopsy. The test came back positive. It was later determined that the blood that I received in 1979, when I was shot, was tainted with the virus. At that time, there was no screening for HCV. I was scheduled for treatment for the infection but there is no cure. I was given three injections a week for one year, plus Ribavirin, which is an antiviral medicine. Six months into the treatment, (the treatment was supposed to be for a year) the doctor said that the medicines were not working but that he wanted to continue for the remaining six months to see what would happen.

On one particular visit, I was impressed by the Lord to ask the nurse about my blood work. This was something I had never done. She said that she was going to talk to me about it after giving me the injections because the reports did not look right. She said my viral load and my liver enzymes were almost normal. About a month or so before that particular visit to the doctors, Pastor Diana Lyles called and asked me if I could give her aunt a ride home to Lakewood, New Jersey. When I arrived at my Leader's home, I was barely inside the door before her aunt grabbed me and laid hands on my stomach. She prophesied that the Lord was giving me a new organ. Only through the Holy Ghost was that revealed. She did not know that I was believing God for my total healing. If God can keep a bullet from killing me and bring a twisted face back to normal, He could give me a new liver. It is a blessing to serve leadership.

It is very important that we make ourselves available to anointed leadership to help when we are called upon. I would have missed my blessing had I not been willing to serve and to do so with a cheerful heart.

To those of you reading this and need a healing,
I SPEAK HEALING TO YOU RIGHT NOW, IN THE NAME OF JESUS. I SPEAK TO EVERY ORGAN, BLOOD CELL, MARROW OF THE BONE, OXYGEN LEVEL, KNEES, JOINTS, BLOOD CIRCULATION, EVERY PART OF YOUR BODY, I COMMAND YOU TO OPERATE AND LINE UP WITH THE WORD OF GOD. BE HEALED, ACCEPT NOTHING LESS. YOU HAVE A COVENANT RIGHT TO IT. IT'S YOURS, IN JESUS' NAME.

Remember, Jeremiah 32:27 KJV - He is the God of all flesh and there is nothing too hard for Him, adapted from. This is a good place to give God praise for your healing, **Isaiah 53:5 KJV – But He was wounded for our transgressions, he was bruised for our iniquities: the chastisement of our peace was upon Him; and with His stripes we are healed.**

ANYONE CAN BE HEALED

I want you to know, that I do not have any problems with my liver. In September 2003, my doctor ordered a follow-up biopsy and it came back with no scaring on the liver (meaning no liver disease). Again, God moved and stayed the hand of death against a disease that could have killed me. **Lamentations 3:22 KJV – It is of the Lord's mercies that we are not consumed, because his compassions fail not.** They are new every morning: Great is thy faithfulness, unto me. Morning by morning, new mercies I see. Thank you Lord for loving me that much.

CECELIA WOODARD

9

DELIVERANCE WITHOUT A TRACE

In the summer of 1989, I met and witnessed to my late husband, Bradford Woodard. At that time he was heavily into cocaine. He was high on cocaine and wanted to go out on a date. I told him that I was a Christian and could not go out with him. So then he asked if we could go for a walk. I told him that if we went for a walk, I would only talk to him about Jesus. Off to the Boardwalk we went. I witnessed to him about the Lord and his marvelous goodness. We must have talked for about four hours. When the Holy Ghost finished, (I had asked the Lord to give me the words to say). Bradford threw his cocaine into the ocean. After leaving the Boardwalk, he asked me to call him and talk to him more about the Lord. I did not call or see him again for quite some time. Whenever I ran into him on the street, I would always encourage him to give his life fully to the Lord. This went on for about a year. I regret to say, at that time he did not stop doing cocaine. But God had a ram in the bush, his brother, Roy Woodard, who has since gone on to be with the Lord.

One day I saw his brother Roy, who had gotten saved and shared with me that Bradford had given his life to the Lord and to call him. I did not call him but I did pray for him to be totally delivered. As God would have it, the next time I saw Bradford, he was on his way to church. He shared his testimony and told me how after hearing the Word of God at a revival, his

ANYONE CAN BE HEALED

brother Roy had invited him to, he had given his life to the Lord and was not looking back. A week later he called and invited me to church with him.

From the day Bradford gave his life to the Lord, until the day he went home to be with the Lord, he did not look back. He did not go through any twelve-step program; the only program that he went to, was the program of the Lord Jesus Christ. **John 8:36 KJV - If the Son therefore shall make you free, ye shall be free indeed.**

In 1994, my husband kept getting sick and seemed to keep a cold. It was during one of his bouts with a cold, that I rushed him to the hospital. Because he was so sick, he was admitted that night. After a week of testing, the doctor called me and asked me to come to his office. The doctor asked me, when was the last time that I had been with my husband sexually. He then explained that my husband was in the last stage of full blown AIDS. He told me that I needed to get tested. I called my doctor who had treated me for the Hepatitis and requested the test. The next day, I went in and the test was administered. After the three-day wait, the nurse called. A peace came over me that I cannot explain. She told me that the results were **NEGATIVE**. God truly gives you peace that is unexplainable. She advised me to have another test done in three months. After hanging up the phone, I went into the ladies' room at work and gave God some serious praise and worship. Once again His goodness, mercy and grace were with me. Once again, He had shown me who He was. After the THREE months were up, I was retested. The results were the same: **NEGATIVE**. I was told to come back in six months, again the results were **NEGATIVE**. I was told to come back in a year, again the results were **NEGATIVE**. I was told to come back the following year, once again **NEGATIVE**. I was told to come back the third and final year, the results once again **NEGATIVE!**

I cannot explain why the Lord did it; He just did it. **Psalm 8:4(a) KJV - What is man, that thou are mindful of him?**

I walked around in awe and still do, at the power of God that He thought enough of me to get into the body fluid. When my husband and I were together as man and wife, the only thing that was being ejaculated into me was straight-up infection. Remember, my husband was in the last stage of full blown AIDS. But God kept my body free from sickness and disease.

I THANK GOD FOR DELIVERANCE WITHOUT A TRACE.

Psalm 103:1-4 KJV - Bless the Lord, O my soul: and all that is within me, bless His Holy name. Bless the Lord, O my soul, and forget not all his benefits: Who forgiveth all thine iniquities; who healeth all thy diseases; Who redeemeth thy life from destruction; who crowneth thee with loving-kindness and tender mercies; (verses 10-12) He hath not dealt with us after our sins; nor rewarded us according to our iniquities. For as the heaven is high above the earth, so great is His mercy toward them that fear Him. As far as the east is from the west, so far hath he removed our transgressions from us.

ANYONE CAN BE HEALED

After reading this story or testimony of just a small part of my life, I pray that someone who needed a boost to their faith, a healing in their body or a change in their situation has received that and more. Because what the Lord has done for me, He will do for you. No matter what the situation is, God can and will fix it. For it is the anointing that destroys the yoke.

When the devil gets on your back, pick up this book and tell him:

**I AM DELIVERED WITHOUT A TRACE
FOR MY GOD HAS FORGIVEN ALL OF MY INIQUITIES AND
HAS HEALED ALL OF MY DISEASES!**

CECELIA WOODARD

Read **Mark 5:15 - The man that was possessed with devils, was sitting at the feet of Jesus clothed and in his right mind.**

HE WAS DELIVERED WITHOUT A TRACE...GOD HAS NO RESPECT OF PERSONS. GET YOUR DELIVERANCE.

AS OF APRIL 22, 2012 I AM HEPATITIS FREE. THE TREATMENT WORKED. I HAVE TO COMPLETE THE TREATMENT UNTIL THE END OF OCTOBER. I GIVE ALL GLORY AND PRAISE TO JEHOVAN-REPHEKA, THE LORD MY HEALER. BECAUSE IT WAS HIM AND HIM ALONE THAT ALLOWED THE TREATMENT TO WORK. IT TOOK FROM 1979 UNTIL 2012 TO RECEIVE MY HEALING. BUT GOD! BUT GOD! BUT GOD!

NOW I UNDERSTAND WHY I COULD NOT SEND MY BOOK TO THE PUBLISHER, I HAD TO WAIT ON MY HEALING. NOW THE BOOK IS COMPLETE! GLORY TO GOD!

TESTIMONIALS

OF

HEALINGS

CECELIA WOODARD

The same way God delivered me, He has delivered so many others. These are some of the miraculous healings God has blessed me to be a part of. I am humbled and in complete awe of His wonder working power.

I was having severe waist pain. I went to the hospital for testing and was told that my bones were growing too big and that is why I was having the pain. The pains radiated right down my left leg. I had suffered with this severe discomfort for many years. But when Prophetess Cecelia Woodard prayed for me, I was instantly healed, and now I have no waist pain.

Mengue Marie Jeanne

ANYONE CAN BE HEALED

I was having bad pains in my ears, serious toothache and headaches. The infection was very bad. The doctor was to operate on my mouth. But when Prophetess Cecelia Woodard prayed on me, I was totally healed. When I went to see the doctor for the operation, I was told I have no problem with my teeth. Praise the Lord for healing me.

Christelle Makousting

CECELIA WOODARD

My name is Mrs. Marie Mbog. I had swollen leg disease, but when the Prophetess prayed for me, I received an instant healing. I am grateful to God for her obedience to come to Cameroon. I was in debt of 700,000F CFA ($1,400.00 American dollars). But I heard the Prophetess preach about a widow who the Lord used. God's servant Elisha performed a miracle that enabled the widow to clear her debt. After prayer, I went home. The following day someone came and paid the debt he owed me which allowed me to clear all my debt.

Also, I was in an accident that left a hole on top of my head.

For over 10 years the doctors could not heal the hole. I had to keep my head bandaged daily to keep out infection. The woman of God called me out and said she did not know why, but that God told her to lay hands on my head. Two days later jelly like skin covered the hole. When I showed the doctors they didn't know what to make of it. God is a miracle God.

Marie Mbog

ANYONE CAN BE HEALED

THESE TESTIMONIES THAT YOU HAVE JUST READ ARE JUST A FEW FROM THE 2007 CRUSADE IN YAOUNDA, CAMEROON, WEST AFRICA. THERE WERE TOO MANY TO PUT IN THIS ONE BOOK. **REMEMBER . . . GOD HAS NO RESPECT OF PERSONS. GET YOUR DELIVERANCE.**

CECELIA WOODARD

My Instant Healing

In December 2008, I was attending a beautiful and powerful service at Victory First Presbyterian Deliverance Church in Atlantic City, New Jersey. I was really enjoying myself in the Lord, when without warning my tooth began to ache with excruciating pain! I tried taking Tylenol and Ibuprofen. After a while, realizing nothing was working, I headed to the bathroom to swish my mouth with salt water. On the way, I almost passed out and asked the Lord to help me make it to the bathroom. The pain was just that bad. Prophetess Woodard was in the bathroom and overheard me telling someone how bad my tooth was hurting. She approached me, and asked me if she could pray for me. No sooner than she touched my left cheek, very gently, the pain began to leave...instantly! She prayed a prayer of power with such peace and assurance of faith. When she finished praying, my tooth was healed, the pain was gone. I had struggled with the pain in my tooth since July 2007. It is February 2009, and I still have no pain.

What an amazing God that we serve. He is even mindful of a toothache. I thank God for the mighty vessel that he used that night in the bathroom of Victory First Presbyterian Deliverance Church. I thank God for her obedience and willingness to pray for me, a stranger in pain in the bathroom of her church.

Thank you and God bless you Prophetess for your prayer.

Miss Crystal Hackley
Egg Harbor, NJ

ANYONE CAN BE HEALED

First, I want to thank God for this opportunity to be a witness for His miraculous healing power. I received both physical and spiritual healings. A week before the arrival of Prophetess Woodard, I had prayed to God for a move of God in my life. I needed help from the Lord like yesterday! I received a call from a friend of mine in Meridian, Mississippi, that a Prophetess was coming from New Jersey, to a church in Meridian. This was March 2010. I was so excited; I could hardly wait for the first night. Because I live 99 miles away in Tuscaloosa, Alabama, I made preparations to stay overnight. On the first night of the service, Pastor Woodard prayed for me. I went down in the Spirit of the Lord. She continued to hover over me speaking what the Lord was saying. I don't remember the words that she spoke, but I remember the power of the words. I was, without a doubt, in the presence of the Lord. I was unable to speak or move. Eventually, as I was helped up, I all but hobbled back to my seat rejoicing in what the Lord had done. My plan was to go home the next day (Friday), but as the Lord would have it, I was there for the Saturday morning service. We had another powerful service. Once again, I found myself in the prayer line, and once again I was out in the Spirit of the Lord.

The Lord was working on me little by little. The news came that Prophetess would also be there on Sunday, which was not her original schedule. The move of God was so strong no one wanted her to leave. We were all hungry for more… I know I was. That Sunday, it all came together: the day of my total healing. Due to a severe infection, my ears had been blocked. When I walked, I would stumble, walk sideways or crooked because my balance was off due to the ear infection. At times I could not see straight, as if confused because of the dizziness, which was quite frequent and disturbing. It was at those times that I felt vulnerable to falling or passing out. That Sunday was a day of complete healing for me. At the time of my healing, I felt a popping sensation in my ears that was painful.

Even though the power of God's presence was "ear splitting", I could hear Prophetess Woodard ever so clearly as she spoke to my ears and commanded them to open. The healing was immediate. Later that evening after getting back to my hotel room, I noticed that the noise from the television was either too loud or my hearing was exceptional. I had to keep adjusting the volume control from channel to channel. At one point, I

CECELIA WOODARD

asked myself, "What is wrong with the television?" That is when I REMEMBERED it wasn't the television! My hearing had been totally restored. My hearing had been fine-tuned!

Again, I received yet another phone call from a friend saying, Prophetess Woodard had been held over at another church. Of course, I went. At that service, because I had been in the prayer line at two different services and received so much from the Lord already, I did not want to get in the line again. I heard the Lord say to me, stand where you are and I will complete your healing. So I reached out to Him, thanking Him for the rest of my healing. The next morning I noticed that as I walked the pain was all but gone. Over the next two or three days there was no pain. I was in "healing shock", if there is such a thing. I had suffered doctor after doctor. Creams, shots, traction. Literally spent thousands of dollars on podiatrists, neurologist, and Emergency rooms. You name it, I tried it. I had stopped going to the chiropractor because the pain had not abated at all. After the healing in March, I went to see the chiropractor and announced that I was healed. It was a setup from God from beginning to end for my healing.

I sincerely thank Prophetess Woodard for allowing the Lord to use her.

Dorothy M. Davis

ANYONE CAN BE HEALED

VICTORY

OVER

FEAR

SCRIPTURES

CECELIA WOODARD

Psalm 56:3-4 Whenever I am afraid, I will trust in You. In God (I will praise His word), In God I have put my trust; I will not fear what flesh can do unto me.

2 Timothy 1:7 For God has not given us a spirit of fear, but of power and of love and of a sound mind.

Romans 8:15 For you did not receive the spirit of bondage again to fear; but you received the Spirit of adoption, by whom we cry out, "Abba, Father."

John 14:1 "Let not your heart be troubled: you believe in God, believe also in Me.

Psalm 27:1-3 The Lord is my light and my salvation; Whom shall I fear? The Lord is the strength of my life; of whom shall I be afraid? When the wicked, came against me to eat up my flesh, my enemies and foes, they stumbled and fell. Though an army may encamp against me, my heart shall not fear; though war should rise against me, in this I will be confident.

Psalm 9:9-10 The Lord also will be a refuge for the oppressed, a refuge in times of trouble. And those who know Your name will put their trust in You; For You, Lord, have not forsaken those who seek You.

Psalm 42:5 Why are you cast down, O my soul? And why are you disquieted within me? Hope in God, for I shall yet praise Him for the help of His countenance.

Psalms 146:8 The Lord opens the eyes of the blind; The Lord raises those who are bowed down; The Lord loves the righteous.

ANYONE CAN BE HEALED

Ephesians 4:23-24 And be renewed in the spirit of your mind, and that you put on the new man, which was created according to God, in true righteousness and holiness.

Philippians 2:5 Let this mind be in you, which was also in Christ Jesus.

CECELIA WOODARD

SCRIPTURES

FOR

HEALING

ANYONE CAN BE HEALED

Exodus 23:25 So you shall serve the Lord your God and He will bless your bread and your water; and I will take sickness way from the midst of you.

Psalms 91:10 No evil shall befall you, nor shall any plague come near your dwelling;

Psalm 139:14 I will praise You; for I am fearfully and wonderfully made; Marvelous are your works, and that my soul knows very well.

Psalm 119:28 My soul melts from heaviness; strengthen me according to Your word.

Psalm 27:1-2 The Lord is my light and my salvation; whom shall I fear? The Lord is the strength of my life; of whom shall I be afraid? When the wicked came against me to eat up my flesh, my enemies and foes, they stumbled and fell.

Psalms 107:20 He sent His word and healed them, and delivered them from their destructions.

Malachi 4:2 But to you who fear My name The Sun of Righteousness shall arise with healing in His wings; and you shall go out and grow fat like stall-fed calves.

James 5:15 And the prayer of faith will save the sick, and the Lord will raise him up; and if he has committed sins, he will be forgiven.

Job 33:25 His flesh shall be young like a child's, He shall return to the days of his youth.

Matthew 8:17 That it might be fulfilled which was spoken by Isaiah the prophet, saying: "He Himself took our infirmities and bore our sicknesses."

CECELIA WOODARD

Isaiah 53:5 But He was wounded for our transgressions, He was bruised for our iniquities; the chastisement for our peace was upon Him, and by His stripes we are healed.

Romans 8:11 But if the Spirit of Him who raised Jesus from the dead dwells in you, He who raised Christ from the dead will also give life to your mortal bodies through His Spirit who dwells in you.

NOTES

SECTION

CECELIA WOODARD

ANYONE CAN BE HEALED

CECELIA WOODARD

ANYONE CAN BE HEALED

CECELIA WOODARD

My Bishop Dr. Charles R. Lyles
@
Victory First Presbyterian Deliverance Church
Atlantic City, New Jersey

ANYONE CAN BE HEALED

My Pastor Dr. Diana L. Lyles,
DLM MINISTRIES INTERNATIONAL
@
Victory First Presbyterian Deliverance Church
Atlantic City, New Jersey

CECELIA WOODARD

My mom(in the spirit) Ernestine Turner
Chief Prophetess Sheila "Favor" Pittman
Apostle Cecelia Woodard
@
The Rock Church International
Humble, Texas

ANYONE CAN BE HEALED

Chief Prophetess Sheila "Favor" Pittman
Apostle Cecelia Woodard
Chief Apostle David Pittman
@
Rock Church International,
Humble, Texas

CECELIA WOODARD

To contact the author write:

Cecelia Woodard
W.I.N. Internatinal Ministries
5880 Ridgewood Road, Suite I-79
Jackson, Mississippi 39211

Please include your testimony as to how this book influenced your faith.

All prayer requests are welcomed.

Internet Address
Winminstries.webs.com

ANYONE CAN BE HEALED

**PROPHETESS
CECELIA WOODARD**

CECELIA WOODARD

Exodus 23:25 KJV

[25] And ye shall serve the LORD your God, and he shall bless thy bread, and thy water; and I will take sickness away from the midst of thee.

EAT YOUR PORTION AND BE HEALED
IN THE
MATCHLESS, MIGHTY
NAME of JESUS

ANYONE CAN BE HEALED

ABOUT THE AUTHOR

I Cecelia Woodard was born in December, the only child of Jean Ragland-Webster and Benjamin Bow, and was raised in Atlantic City, New Jersey. She is the mother of one son, Eugene Ragland, the grandmother of two grandsons, Courtney Younger and Donte Belcher, and one granddaughter, Isis Ragland, who are her gifts from God.

Prophetess Woodard received the baptism of the Holy Ghost in July 1979 under the leadership of Pastor Loretta Farmer.

In June of 1980, Prophetess Cecelia Woodard moved to Philadelphia, Pennsylvania where she became a member of the Act of Apostles Church under the leadership of Bishop and Elder Gantt. It was during this time in her life that she received her call to the ministry and the prophetic gift in her life was refined. As God would have it, in 1984, Prophetess Woodard was directed to become a member of the Greater Works Ministry where she was cultivated and prepared by Apostle Ruth Jackson to go forth and preach the Word of God.

In 1988, Prophetess Woodard returned to Atlantic City and upon finding a fellowship to call home, she became a member, and after much impartation, a daughter of Victory First Presbyterian Deliverance Church under the auspices of Bishop Charles R. Lyles and Pastor Diana L. Lyles. It was under this ministry that she became an ordained Evangelist and worked in her gifts and calling.

In June of 1997, Prophetess Woodard was afforded the opportunity to travel to London, England. In January 1998 – February 1999, God used her to pour out His manifestation upon His people in Abidjan, West Africa, Ivory Coast.

It was during the year of 2003, that the Lord planted Prophetess Woodard in Dayton, Ohio. While asking the Lord one night in prayer, what was her purpose in Dayton, the Lord began to deal with her about Woodard Ministries. After much prayer, Woodard Ministries was born in

CECELIA WOODARD

September of 2005.

She began Bible Study at the YWCA. While ministering there, women were delivered from crack cocaine, prostitution and from being homeless. Their self-esteem and self-worth were given back to them through the Word of God. Many who were on drugs and homeless are now saved, Holy Ghost-filled, attending various ministries and no longer living on the streets.

After seeking the Lord's face or a church home in which to worship, she was led to Charity and Faith Thru Jesus Christ Sanctuary ministry. There she served under the dynamic leadership of Pastors Liz and Warner Taylor.

In March of 2007, Prophetess Woodard was blessed with the opportunity to minister in Yaounde, Cameroon, West Africa for eighteen days. During that crusade, the outpouring of the Lord was so great that 200 souls were saved and healed. In addition, there were miracles, signs and wonders following. It was during this move of God that WIN – Woodard International Ministries was birthed.

Prophetess Woodard is the General Overseer of the Christ Gospel International Church in Yaounde, Cameroon, West Africa, which has over 200 members and is still growing. There are also six other churches under her leadership in Cameroon, West Africa. Used under the anointing of God, she has documented medical miracles, many of which occurred in Africa.

After returning from Africa, the Lord saw fit to add Daddy God Ministries, located in Orange County, California to WIN International Ministries.

At the leading of the Lord, September of 2007, Prophetess Woodard returned to Atlantic City, New Jersey and continues to sit under the auspices of Bishop Charles R. Lyles and Pastor Diana L. Lyles, working in her gifts and callings.

June 2009, Pastor Cecelia Woodard ministered under the anointing at San Jose, Costa Rica.

ANYONE CAN BE HEALED

August 2010, the Lord yet again transitioned Prophetess Cecelia Woodard. This transaction moved her to Meridian, Mississippi where she set up a Bible study, and souls were healed and delivered.

May of 2011, the Lord enlarged her tent, to Jackson, Mississippi where she now Pastors. In November 2012 – December 2012, Apostle Cecelia Woodard ministered for one month in Nigeria, Abia State, where strong deliverance took place. Shortly after her return to America in December 2012, Apostle Cecelia Woodard traveled to Santo Domingo and San Christobia. Dominican Republic in January 2013, where God once again moved in Miracles, signs and wonders.

April 2011, Prophetess Woodard received her Doctor of Divinity Degree. In June 2013, she received her Degree in Theology from Wayside Bible College in Clinton, Mississippi.

Used under the anointing of God, she has documented miracles, many of which are in Africa. She gives Glory and Honor to God for all He has done.

CECELIA WOODARD

ANYONE CAN BE HEALED

ORDER FORM

Send me _____ copies of "Anyone Can Be Healed

@15.00 each $_____
Subtotal $_____
Add sales tax
According to
Your state $_____
Name_____
Address_____
City_____
State_____ Zip Code_____
Daytime Phone:_____
Evening Phone:_____
E-Mail:_____
Make all Checks/Money orders payable to:

Cecelia Woodard
5880 Ridgewood Road, Suite I-79
Jackson, Mississippi 39211
Woodard1510@yahoo.com

CECELIA WOODARD

www.ingramcontent.com/pod-product-compliance
Lightning Source LLC
Chambersburg PA
CBHW041403090426
42743CB00006B/140